Mike

Enjoy !!

Countdown to West Virginia Statehood

Bob O'Connor

By Bob O'Connor

∾ INFINITY
PUBLISHING

Copyright © 2013 by Bob O'Connor
Cover graphic – abrahamlincolnclassroom.org

ISBN 978-0-7414-8312-6

Printed in the United States of America

Published February 2013

INFINITY PUBLISHING
1094 New DeHaven Street, Suite 100
West Conshohocken, PA 19428-2713
Toll-free (877) BUY BOOK
Local Phone (610) 941-9999
Fax (610) 941-9959
Info@buybooksontheweb.com
www.buybooksontheweb.com

Other books by Bob O'Connor

"The Perfect Steel Trap Harpers Ferry 1859"

"The Virginian Who Might Have Saved Lincoln"

"Catesby: Eyewitness to the Civil War"

"The US Colored Troops at Andersonville Prison"

"The Centennial History of Ranson WV -- 1910 – 2010"

"The Life of Abraham Lincoln: As President"

"A House Divided Against Itself"

"The Return of Catesby"

www.boboconnorbooks.com

Dedication

In the early 1800s, already two factions had been
recognized dividing Virginia into "the planters"
and "the mountaineers".
This book is dedicated to the pioneer spirit that has
always been exemplified by the people of what is today West
Virginia. To me, those that best exemplify that "mountaineer
spirit" today include people like NBA and college Hall of
Fame basketball player Jerry West; high school, college and
National Football League Hall of Fame football player Sam
Huff; Olympic champion Mary Lou Retton; Grammy award
winning country singer Kathy Mattea; United State Senator
Robert Byrd; Nobel Prize winning author Pearl S. Buck;
former Prisoner of War Jessica Lynch; teachers Jim Taylor
and Bill Jordan; West Virginia coal miners;
and many others.
That spirit cannot be taught. Some obviously were born
with it. Some of us who have just moved here recently
have been fortunate to find it and embrace it.
If you don't understand what "mountaineer spirit" is,
no explanation would suffice. If you do understand,
no explanation is necessary.
My hats off to those who exemplify
the "mountaineer spirit".

Foreword

This book grew out of a series of 27 articles I wrote for several newspapers in West Virginia that will run from the first week in January 2013 through and past the 150th birthday of the state on June 20, 2013. I was trying to provide a concise explanation of the long and arduous process which led to the formation of the state of West Virginia where I live.

People in general think the state of West Virginia was the immediate reaction to the secession of Virginia in 1861, a move many western Virginians did not support. The division of the two sections of Virginia (the planters vs. the mountaineers as Henry Howe called them) can actually be traced back to the original Commonwealth of Virginia constitution of 1776. Due to that first document, many western Virginians were not able to vote because of a requirement of land ownership.

The result was that the eastern representatives in the General Assembly lorded over their western counterparts for years and years. And that didn't sit well at all with the mountaineers who have always been a proud people, sticking up for their rights long before they had their own state.

Historians and legal experts argue, even today, that the formation of West Virginia was illegal and unconstitutional. But the United States Supreme Court ruled just the opposite.

When you are finished with this book, I think you will have a much greater understanding of the interesting process and the outstanding characters that banded together to form the new state of West Virginia.

June 20, 2013. Happy Birthday, West Virginia. As West Virginia Metronews sportscaster Tony Caridi would say, "It is a great day to be a mountaineer."

Part I

Chapter 1
The Fairfax land grant

Statehood for West Virginia was a long, hard road. In spite of popular belief to the contrary, the countdown to statehood and the western part of the state's problems with the rest of the state didn't start with the American Civil War. It started long before that.

Western Virginia was originally part of almost 6 million acres acquired in 1718 by Thomas Fairfax, the 6th Lord Fairfax of Cameron. Lord Fairfax's huge land grants [1] contained all the land between the mouth of the Potomac River and the mouth of the Rappahannock River.

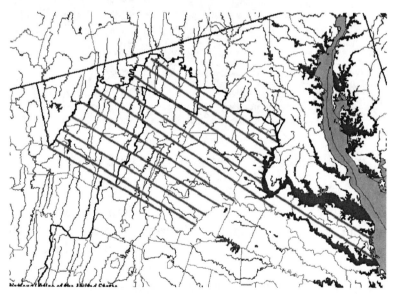

Lord Fairfax land grants showing today's political boundaries
http://www.virginiaplaces.org/settleland/fairfaxgrant.html

---

[1]   http://www.virginiaplaces.org/settleland/fairfaxgrant.html

In order to start selling his vast holdings, Lord Fairfax needed the huge acreage to be divided into smaller, more saleable plats. His land was formally subdivided by various surveyors, including a young George Washington, over a span of several years. Among those new first residents were German immigrants who settled in Mecklenberg (today known as Shepherdstown) in 1727.

By 1746, a stone was set called the Fairfax Stone (located today in Fairfax Stone Historical Monument State Park[2] at the convergence of Tucker and Preston Counties) to identify the Lord Fairfax parcel.

Fairfax Stone
Source: virginiaplaces.org/settleland/fairfaxgrant.html

During the early 1750s, some settlers began crossing the mountains into western Virginia. Their journeys were often impeded and discouraged by Native Americans. A larger group started immigrating after the American Revolution.

In the latter stages of the 1700s, towns had sprung up in what today is known as the eastern panhandle -- Morgan, Berkeley and Jefferson Counties. Western Virginia was settled later, due to the aforementioned problems with the

---

[2] www.westvirginiastateparks.com

local Native American and conflicting land disputes that took years to settle in the courts.

From the beginning, there were both physical and psychological differences from the two ends of the state, separated physically by the Allegheny Mountains. Whereas their eastern Virginia neighbors owned plantations, raised tobacco with slave labor, and relied on the sea for its commerce, those who lived in western Virginia owned much smaller acreage and found slavery not to be profitable. Eastern Virginians tended to face the Atlantic Ocean while their western counterparts traded more toward the Ohio and Mississippi Rivers.

As the years went by, the western section of the state increased in population more rapidly than their eastern counterparts, but their neighbors to the east always had the political advantage laid out in the state's constitutions.

The 1790's census shows the total population of eastern and western Virginia to have been 750,000 with only 55,000 living in the western region.[3] The eastern section had thirteen times more people giving them a huge advantage in the General Assembly.

By 1820, Virginia's seaside population numbers had grown, but the western region was growing significantly faster.[4] Still the eastern plurality was six to one. Forty years later, in 1860, the western region continued growing at a much faster rate, cutting the east's majority to three to one.[5] But even with the increase in population, western Virginia's representatives in the General Assembly got very little support from their eastern Virginia brethren.

---

[3] http://www.virginiaplaces.org/population/pop1790numbers.html
[4] http://www.virginiaplaces.org/population/pop1820numbers.html
[5] http://www.virginiaplaces.org/population/pop1860numbers.html

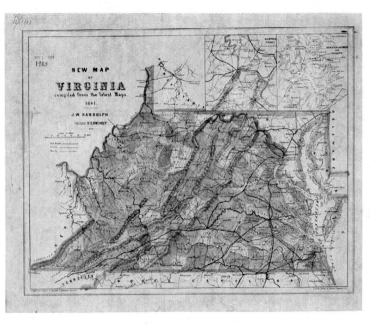

Map of Virginia 1861   Source: virginiamemory.com

Chapter 2
The planters vs. the mountaineers

There has always been a wide split over many issues between those who lived in eastern Virginia and their counterparts in western Virginia. Those differences were deep and long established and eventually were the reasons for the formation of the new state of West Virginia in 1863.

Eastern Virginians always tended to be farmers and planters, operating on large plantations and utilizing their free slave labor. Western Virginians had much smaller areas to grow crops. They farmed their own land as slavery was not a profitable venture.

The 1860 Slave map of Virginia [6] shows a huge difference in slave populations between the two sections. If you look at the percentage of slaves as part of the county population in all of Virginia, of the highest eighty-two counties, only one, Jefferson County, was from the western section. Jefferson County had 3,960 slaves making up 28.2 percent of their population. By comparison, 37 eastern counties had a higher percentage of slaves than whites.

In total, the 105 eastern Virginia counties had about 480,000 slaves while the western Virginia counties had only 17,622 slaves. Henrico County in eastern Virginia had more slaves than the entire western Virginia region.

Only six of western Virginia's counties had more than 1,000 slaves (Jefferson, Kanawha, Berkeley, Greenbrier, Hardy and Hampshire Counties). By comparison, in eastern Virginia, 40 counties had more than 5,000 slaves. In fact, 11 eastern Virginia counties each had more than 10,000 slaves.

The 1820 census[7] shows a total Virginia population of approximately 1 million with about 140,000 living in what is

---

[6] http://www.sonofthesouth.net/slavery/slave-maps/virginia-slave-map.htm

[7] http://www.virginiaplaces.org/population/pop1820numbers.html

today West Virginia. In thirty years, the seaside of the state had increased its population by one third, while the western end had nearly tripled in population. The eastern Virginia advantage had dwindled to having six times more people. But the plurality was still significant in hindering any attempts by the western delegates to get any of their favorable legislation passed.

In the 1860 census [8] the eastern counties had over 700,000 whites and nearly 480,000 slaves, for a total population of almost 1.2 million. The western region statistics showed 340,000 white settlers along with only about 18,000 slaves, for a total of just under 360,000 people. Slavery was a staple form of commerce on one side of the state and was virtually an insignificant form of commerce at the opposite end which today is called West Virginia.

The Allegheny Mountains in between the two factions created a physical barrier that kept the two areas quite separate on most all matters.

Henry Howe depicted the differences between the factions in his "Historical Collections of Virginia 1816 – 1893" published in 1923. He called those who lived in eastern Virginia "planters" and those who lived in western Virginia "mountaineers." Howe realized the differences included social, political and economic elements.

[8]   http://www.virginiaplaces.org/population/pop1860numbers.html

LIFE IN EASTERN VIRGINIA.
The Home of the Planter.

LIFE IN WESTERN VIRGINIA.
The Home of the Mountaineer.

"Historical Collections of Virginia 1816 – 1893"
by Henry Howe
Published in 1923
Source: <u>washingtonpost.com</u>

Chapter 3
Virginia's first constitution -- 1776

The long road to West Virginia's statehood took on a totally different meaning when the first constitution of the Commonwealth of Virginia was signed on June 12, 1776.

The constitution was mostly penned by George Mason. It was ratified by the Constitutional Convention delegates and, as happened in many of the country's new colonies, was not subject to the approval of voters across the state.

An absolutely critical portion of that first state constitution, as far as those who lived in the western part of the state were concerned, was the provision that gave voting rights to persons who owned at least 25 acres of improved or 50 acres of unimproved land. The Constitution states it this way officially: "that all men, having sufficient evidence of permanent common interest with, and attachment to, the community, have the right of suffrage." This law created discrimination and lesser representation in the western Virginia counties.

The people who lived in western Virginia tended to own smaller plots of land and therefore a large portion of their people couldn't vote. Western Virginia's land mass (24,000 square miles) made up about a third of Virginia's total of 66,000 square miles at the time. Much of the western Virginia acreage was wild, difficult to be tilled and farmed, or in mountainous areas. The terms "planters" versus "mountaineers" emerged from those contrasting life styles.

Eastern Virginia always maintained a huge majority of landowners and thereby of potentially eligible voters. Western Virginia's representatives to the state's General Assembly never had enough votes on their own to affect the legislation they needed. Their pleas of equal representation fell on the deaf ears of the legislative majority.

Thomas Jefferson had noted the constitution's seeming tendency to concentrate arbitrary power in the legislature and ignoring the minority's wishes (the minority being western Virginia). In his *Notes on the State of Virginia* written in 1784, Jefferson[9] addressed the issue as follows: The concentration of government power in the general assembly "is precisely the definition of despotic government. It will be no alleviation that these powers will be exercised by a plurality of hands, and not a single one. One hundred and seventy-three despots (the number of the Virginia legislators) would surely be as oppressive as one. Let those who doubt it turn their eyes on the republic of Venice — as little will it avail us that they are chosen by ourselves. An *elective despotism* was not the government we fought for, but one which should not only be founded on free principles, but in which the powers of the government should be so divided and balanced among several bodies of magistracy, as that no one could transcend their legal limits, without being effectually checked and restrained by the others."

That first constitution created a fissure between the eastern and western portions of the state. That division was never repaired.

geo. Mason.

George Mason, author of the first Virginia constitution
Source: <u>virtualology.com</u>

---

[9] Notes on the State of Virginia
   etext.virginia.edu/toc/modeng/public/JefVirg.html, Query 13, page 245

Chapter 4
A mountaineer complains about inequality

The differences between western and eastern Virginia continued long after the ink had dried on the first Virginia constitution in 1776.

The state continued to grow and prosper. Although the growth in the west far outdistanced that of the eastern section, it never put a dent in the political differential between the two sections. In the first census (1790),[10] the eastern region showed a thirteen to one population edge, creating much larger representation for their portion of the state. As the plurality decreased to six to one in the 1820 Virginia Census[11] and three to one in the 1860 Census,[12] eastern Virginia still controlled all the actions of the Virginia General Assembly because they still maintained a wide majority of the legislative seats. Eastern Virginia also had twice as many counties as their counterparts.

A western Virginia legislator added fuel to the fire when he wrote a letter to the newspaper in 1803.[13] In his letter to the *Richmond Examiner*, John G. Jackson, a Harrison County delegate, complained about the inequality between the two ends of Virginia. Jackson, writing under the pseudonym "a mountaineer," said that although western Virginians paid property taxes on their land, they had virtually no voting rights.

Jackson reasoned that the Virginia Constitution actually violated the Declaration of Independence because it was "taxation without representation."

Here's part of Jackson's actual letter. "The disfranchisement of all the freemen of Virginia, except those

---

[10] http://www.virginiaplaces.org/population/pop1790numbers.html
[11] http://www.virginiaplaces.org/population/pop1820numbers.html
[12] http://www.virginiaplaces.org/population/pop1860numbers.html
[13] http://www.as.wvu.edu/wvhistory/documents/019.pdf *The Richmond Enquirer*, January 15, 1803

possessing lands, is so impolitic a measure, and so subversive of natural right, that if the constitution were perfect in every other part, it would demand a prompt interference, and decisive change. The late enumeration of appeals the inhabitants of the United States affords a strong argument of it's impolicy; for to what other cause can we attribute the great proportional increase of the white population in those states where that right of suffrage is extended to all citizens paying taxes - and the comparative diminution, in the states, where the right is circumscribed in the narrowest limits...These are strong confirmations of the idea suggested, that the measure is impolitic. That it is subversive of natural right and will not be denied....your civil policy has robbed me of my right of suffrage..."

Those who lived in the western areas agreed with Jackson, sensing all along that the eastern areas dominated the legislature and seemed unwilling to listen to their western wants and needs. And because of the overloaded legislature, western Virginians could never get enough support for their ideas and thus were never able to overcome the odds.

Jackson not only served in the Virginia General Assembly, he also served in the U. S. House of Representatives and as a U. S. District Court Judge from western Virginia. The "mountaineer" died in 1825 at age 47.

With all its flaws, the first Virginia Constitution lasted until April of 1830.

The original response to taxation without representation
The Boston Tea Party
Source: learnnc.org

Chapter 5
Thomas Jefferson suggests change

During the statehood struggle for western Virginia, the year 1816 was a critical one. The perceived inequality on the political scene in Virginia continued to push the two sections of the state further apart, widening the gap.

In 1816, Thomas Jefferson suggested legislative representation be based on the white population, that all free white males be given voting privileges and that state and local officials would be subject to election by the popular vote.

In a letter to Samuel Kercheval,[14] Jefferson said "let it be agreed that a government is republican in proportion as every member composing it has his equal voice in the direction of its concerns (not indeed in person, which would be impracticable beyond the limits of a city, or small township, but) by representatives chosen by himself, and responsible to him at short periods, and let us bring to the test of this canon every branch of our constitution. In the legislature, the House of Representatives is chosen by less than half the people, and not at all in proportion to those who do choose. The Senate is still more disproportionate."

Western Virginia's delegation met to discuss many of those same ideas and to develop their own strategy in the House and Senate chambers. Their convention was held in Staunton in the Shenandoah Valley. Even though the 49 eastern counties had a majority in the legislature, the western counties were growing due to more people moving across the Allegheny Mountains. The Tidewater delegates were not anxious to give up their power – something that they had enjoyed since the commonwealth was founded. That was not sitting well with the western representatives. But the western

---

[14] Letter written on June 12, 1816 --
http://www.as.wvu.edu/wvhistory/documents/019.pdf

Virginia delegates could not agree on any long-term answers to the region's problems.

The General Assembly of the Commonwealth of Virginia did, in fact, pass new legislation that same year. And it was favorable, in some respects, to those who lived in the western reaches of the state. The western region got greater representation with the reapportionment based on the white male population. In addition, the legislative body set up a Board of Public Works. It was to be their charge to develop and/or expand the road and canal systems in western Virginia.

But western Virginians were still feeling discriminated against by the state laws requiring voting rights that were tied to land ownership. Virginia was bucking the national trend in this manner, as it was one of only two states still holding the opinion that regarded land owners as eligible to vote. The state of Pennsylvania had already abolished property requirements for voting in 1776 by allowing adult white men who paid taxes the right to vote.

Representation in the Virginia General Assembly was by county rather than by population. Eastern Virginia had more counties. And western Virginians were also left out in the election of the governor, lieutenant governor, judges, the attorney general and U. S. Senators because they had less representation. Those public officials were still being elected by the Virginia General Assembly rather than by popular vote.

Thomas Jefferson   Source: freewebs.com

Chapter 6
A new constitutional convention is held

The road to West Virginia statehood became a wee bit rockier between 1828 and 1830.

The delegates from western Virginia, not satisfied with the gains that they had made in new legislation approved by the Virginia General Assembly in 1816, called for a Constitutional Convention again in 1829. They wanted revisions or amendments to the constitution that represented their earlier complaints. They sought the vote for all free white males, equal representation based on the white population and the direct election by popular vote of state and local officials.

Only one-third of the white male population of the state could vote due to the restriction of property ownership. The first state constitution (1776) had a provision that gave voting rights exclusively to persons who owned at least 25 acres of improved or 50 acres of unimproved land. And most of those males who did not own enough land and therefore were not eligible to vote lived in the western region.

The Commonwealth of Virginia opened its Constitutional Convention[15] on October 5, 1829. To show the importance of the convention, some of Virginia's most "famous sons" attended. Those prominent men included John Tyler, John Marshal, James Monroe and James Madison. Of the 96 delegates who made up the convention, 18 were from what is today West Virginia. Not surprising, all three of the agenda items on the western delegation's plate were defeated.

When the new state constitution was finally ratified after nearly four months of deliberation, it faced a popular vote throughout the Commonwealth of Virginia. The new document was approved by the people in April, 1830 by a margin of 26,055 to 15,566 (63% to 37%). More than three times as many people voted in the east than the west.

---

[15] http://www.wvculture.org/history/government/182930cc.html

But the final tally didn't show the true colors of the state's two opposing factions. In the western Virginia counties, the vote was in opposition to the new constitution by the count of 8,356 to 1,383 (86% to 14%). By backing out the western vote, the eastern side of the state ratified the new constitution by the slim margin of 17,699 to 14,183 (55% to 45%).

The *Kanawha Republican* newspaper responded almost immediately calling for "secession" of western Virginia. And this was 1830, not 1861. The *Wheeling Gazette* of April, 1830, called for the delegates to meet "to treat with the eastern nabobs for a division of the state - peaceably if we can, forcibly if we must."

An outside observer, Thomas L. Lees of New Jersey, the Linsley Institute president, wrote of the Virginia situation in this manner: "That part of Virginia which borders on the Ohio is rapidly improving in wealth and population; its inhabitants have long been dissatisfied with the selfish policy and the usurpations of the eastern slave holders, whose influence in the legislative body has ever been exerted in the perpetration of an oppressive aristocracy. The people here are very different from those of the eastern part of the state. Industry is much more encouraged and respected; slavery is unpopular, and the few who hold slaves generally treat them well. The time is not far distant when western Virginia will either liberalize the present state government, or separate itself entirely from the Old Dominion." His views were certainly prophetic and only about thirty years before their time.

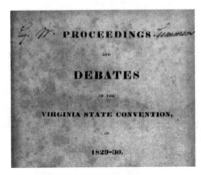

Source: wvculture.org

Chapter 7
The second Virginia constitution is adopted

The second constitution of the Commonwealth of Virginia was ratified by the majority of the voters in April, 1830 replacing the state's original constitution. But it didn't settle the concerns of the western counties of Virginia.

Early 1831 saw an event in Virginia that changed many people's attitudes toward slavery. Nat Turner led a slave rebellion resulting in the massacre of approximately 60 whites. Although the rebellion was squelched, Turner himself was not captured for several months. In the ensuing time period, there was widespread fear amongst the white population across Virginia. Militia and vigilante mobs roamed the commonwealth, rounding up blacks without regard to whether they had actually participated in the rebellion or not. Upwards of 100 or more blacks were executed. State representatives in the South quickly enacted legislation prohibiting coloreds from learning how to read and write and taking away their freedom to assemble.

HORRID MASSACRE IN VIRGINIA·

The Scenes which the above Plate is designed to represent, are—Fig. 1, a Mother intreating for the lives of her children.—2, Mr. Travis, cruelly murdered by his own Slaves.—3. Mr. Barrow, who bravely defended himself against his wife escaped.—4. A comp. of mounted Dragoons in pursuit of the Blacks.

Source: Samuel Warner, *Authentic and impartial narrative of the tragical scene which was witnessed in Southampton County (Virginia)* . . . New York, 1831
Prints and Photographs Division, Library of Congress

Around this same time, William Lloyd Garrison published his newspaper *The Liberator*. He promoted the end of slavery. Western Virginians in many instances became abolitionist because they felt that slaves were taking jobs away from whites.

The 1840's Virginia census [16] showed just how disproportional the state's population was in regard to representation in the General Assembly. In spite of a faster growing population in the western counties, they were represented by only 56 of the 134 delegates and by only 10 of the 29 senators in state government.

By 1840, it was determined by many of the western Virginia leaders that there was a great need for the expansion

---

[16] http://www.virginiaplaces.org/population/pop1840numbers.html

of the railroad. The turnpike and canal projects that had been approved by the legislature were not as satisfactory as previously had been anticipated. Rail transportation promised not only great capacity but a shortened time for getting their products to market. On November 5, 1842, the Baltimore and Ohio Railroad had reached Cumberland, Maryland enroute to the Ohio River. A competition ensued with both Parkersburg and Wheeling vying to become the railroad's westernmost terminus.

A decision on the Baltimore and Ohio Railroad terminus was finally settled in 1847. The Virginia General Assembly chose Wheeling. The route selected would take the railroad through Grafton and Fairmont on the way to Wheeling.

Parkersburg was not totally left out. The Parkersburg representatives chose to build a short line railroad off the main Baltimore and Ohio Railroad tracks to Parkersburg. The project was dubbed the Northwestern Virginia Railroad.

The hundred mile short line railroad, begun in 1852, was completed in five years. By the time the route was completed, the Baltimore and Ohio Railroad had purchased enough bonds of the Northwestern Virginia Railroad that they owned the majority of its financial interests.

Henry Ruffner, President of Washington College, took to the speaker's platform at the Franklin Society meeting in Lexington, Virginia in 1847 to argue against slavery in the trans-Allegheny Virginia area. Ruffner was himself a slave owner and the son of a Kanawha Valley salt industrialist. His speech called for the ending of slavery in the Trans-Allegheny Virginia region in order to provide for more paying jobs for white workers. He theorized that slavery kept white laborers from moving into that area.

Baltimore and Ohio Railroad – circa 1830
Source: scripophily.net

Chapter 8

All Virginian men (age 21) can now vote

In spite of repeated calls for another Constitutional Convention by the western counties, the 1831 constitution prevailed. It wasn't until March 4, 1850 that the General Assembly passed a new convention bill. Ten thousand copies of the bill were circulated throughout the state. The state's voters finally spoke, approving a referendum for a Constitutional Convention by a wide margin.

The "Reform" Constitutional Convention convened in Richmond, Virginia on October 14, 1850.[17] The delegates haggled for nine months over items such as taxation, internal improvements, land assessments, literacy, and the state's liabilities and debts. They considered many changes to the second state constitution. When the dust cleared, the major victory for the western counties came with reform in the requirements for voting. Previously Virginia clung to the old-fashioned laws that you had to own land to be eligible to vote (already given up by this time by every other state in the nation). This time the convention authorized that every white male who had lived in the state for two years and was at least twenty-one years of age could vote.

Western Virginia delegates heralded the long sought decision with great excitement. It had only taken them 74 years to accomplish their goal (from the first constitution in 1776). On top of that, the convention delegates also agreed to allow for the people to elect their Governor, judges and other officials. For all the years up to that point, those officials were elected by the legislature, which had been top heavy with eastern representation.

Western Virginia delegates accepted a proposal to allow property across the state to be taxed at its total value, with the exception of slaves who would be taxed at a lower rate.

---

[17] http://www.wvhumanities.org/Statehood/reformconvention.htm

Several new faces representing western Virginia who had not been on board for the 1829 Constitutional Convention emerged from the 1850 - 1851 convention. Those new political leaders were Waitman T. Willey, Gideon D. Camden, Charles J. Faulkner, John S. Carlisle, George W. Summers, Joseph Johnson, and Benjamin Smith.

Willey, a Morgantown attorney, became one of the first two West Virginia U. S. Senators. Judge Camden was a federal judge of Randolph County and also had oil interests in the state. Faulkner, an attorney from Martinsburg, had introduced a law in the Virginia General Assembly in 1848 that eventually became the Fugitive Slave Act of 1850.[18]

Carlisle was a Winchester attorney who also served in the U. S. Congress. Mr. Summers was a member of the Virginia General Assembly and then a U. S. Congressman. Joseph Johnson, of Bridgeport, assumed the role of chairman of suffrage during the convention and later was elected as the Governor of Virginia. Benjamin Smith was an attorney who lived in Charleston and served as District Attorney of the Western Virginia district.

The state convention adjourned on August 1, 1851. That same year, voters across the state ratified the third Virginia Constitution by a vote of 75,748 to 11,060 (87% to 13%).

Waitman T. Willey
Source: Library of Congress

---

[18] http://www.nationalcenter.org/FugitiveSlaveAct.html

Chapter 9

The first western Virginia governor is elected

In January, 1852 something happened in the Commonwealth of Virginia that had never happened before in the 76 previous years of the state's existence. A western Virginian, Joseph Johnson[19] of Bridgeport, was elected the Governor of Virginia. The previous 31 governors had all been elected from the eastern counties. Johnson, the Democratic candidate, had won the election by 9,000 votes over George W. Summers, the Whig candidate, of Kanawha County.

Johnson had served in the War of 1812 and was in a company of Virginia riflemen. He had also been a member of the U. S. Congress several different times (1823 - 1827, 1833, 1835 - 1841, and 1845 - 1847). He was an avowed abolitionist in spite of the fact that he was both a state's rights Democrat and a slave owner. He held that blacks should receive equal protection under the laws of the Commonwealth of Virginia and condemned the fugitive slave laws.

Governor Joseph Johnson was inaugurated on January 16, 1852 and served until January 1, 1856. Since the governor had been chosen by popular vote for the first time, it had been the first time the western Virginia people could actually vote for the state's governor. Johnson had become the first Virginia governor ever to be elected by popular vote. He was also the only Virginia governor ever elected from west of the Allegheny Mountains.

Ironically, Johnson himself had been the chairman of the suffrage committee at the Constitutional Convention and had championed the idea that all white men over the age of 21 who had lived in the state for a minimum of two years be allowed to vote. Prior to that convention, only land owners could vote in Virginia. The new law certainly had turned the tide and allowed for a western Virginian to be elected governor.

---

[19] http://www.wvhumanities.org/Statehood/josephjohnson.htm

In his first message to the legislature, he called for the General Assembly to complete the James River and Kanawha Canal and extend the Central Railroad. All of those recommendations were approved.

Perhaps the most interesting event Governor Johnson was involved in during his four years in office occurred in 1853. A nineteen year old medical student at the University of Virginia was convicted of a non-fatal shooting and expelled from the university. The young man was sentenced to serve a year in jail. He studied and read law while incarcerated. On December 23, 1853, he was pardoned by Governor Johnson. The young man who the governor pardoned was John Singleton Mosby who became a very famous Confederate cavalry raider in the American Civil War.

Johnson's home that he built in Bridgeport was called "Oakdale." It is one of the town's best examples of Italianate residential architecture. Today the building, known as the Governor Joseph Johnson House, is on the National Register of Historic Places. It is located at 424 Oakdale Avenue.

The book "Governor Joseph Johnson of Virginia -- A brief sketch of his life and character" published in 1923 chronicles his life. It was reprinted in 2011 by Nabu Press who scanned the original with its imperfections and blurred pages included. It is available on Amazon.com.

Governor Joseph Johnson
Source: alanskitchen.com

Chapter 10
Dred Scot and John Brown enter the fray

Under Governor Johnson's leadership (he served from January 1852 to January 1856), western Virginia got help from the General Assembly on structural improvements including the James River and Kanawha Canal and the extension of the Central Railroad.

After a long period of economic prosperity, in 1857, Virginia's economy was suffering from a depression which was part of a worldwide economic crisis. Historically the time period was called "the Panic of 1857." In western Virginia, the salt industry in the Kanawha Valley failed. Many local factories and mills shut down causing large unemployment.

Along with financial crisis, in March of that same year Supreme Court Justice Roger B. Taney ruled in the *Dred Scot vs. Sandford* case[20] which had reverberating implications throughout the nation. Taney's ruling said, "It is difficult at this day to realize the state of public opinion in regard to that unfortunate race which prevailed in the civilized and enlightened portions of the world at the time of the Declaration of Independence, and when the Constitution of the United States was framed and adopted; but the public history of every European nation displays it in a manner too plain to be mistaken. They had for more than a century before been regarded as beings of an inferior order, and altogether unfit to associate with the white race, either in social or political relations, and so far unfit that they had no rights which the white man was bound to respect." The ruling caused a political split in the country between the free soil and the slavery supporters.

---

[20] http://americancivilwar.com/colored/dred_scott.html

Dred Scot
Source: law.harvard.edu

Justice Roger B. Taney
Source: etc.usf.edu

Major national and international attention was focused on the federal arsenal at Harpers Ferry, Virginia when John Brown captured the facility on October 16, 1859. With all eyes on him after he was captured two days later, the federal government decided to try Brown in Charlestown because court was already in session. Brown and six of his men were tried in the Jefferson County Courthouse for treason, inciting slaves to rebel, and murder. Brown, John Cook, Edwin Coppic, Albert Hazlett, and Aaron Stevens were found guilty as charged and sentenced to be "hanged by the neck until they be dead." The two black raiders, Shields Green and John Copeland, were found innocent of treason. To be convicted, you must first be a citizen. According to the Fugitive Slave Act, coloreds were not citizens. They too were sentenced to hang. Captain Brown was hanged on December 2, 1859. John Cook, Shields Green, John Copeland and Edwin Coppic were hanged on December 16, 1859. Albert Hazlett and Aaron Stevens were hanged on March 16, 1860.[21]

While the event didn't affect the entire state, it certainly brought militia units from the nearby environs to both Harpers Ferry and Charlestown from October 1859 through March of 1860. In fact, during that time, there were more troops in Virginia than had been amassed at any time since the Battle of

---

[21] The Perfect Steel Trap, Harpers Ferry 1859, Infinity Publications, 2006.

Yorktown in the Revolutionary War. It also scared Virginians who did not sleep well thinking about the possibilities of a slave revolt.

Hanging of John Brown December 2, 1859 –
drawing by David Hunter Strother
Source: West Virginia and Regional History Collection,
West Virginia University Libraries

Chapter 11
Abraham Lincoln's election causes concern

The national election, held on November 6, 1860 saw Abraham Lincoln elected President of the Unites States with only 39.8% of the vote. In Virginia, he received just 1,887 votes out of 166,891 cast. The Virginia vote was almost equally split between John Breckinridge, Southern Democratic candidate with 74,325 votes (44.5% of the state's vote) and John Bell, Constitutional Union candidate with 74,481 votes (44.6% of the state's vote).

Of Mr. Lincoln's votes, 1,402 came from counties in western Virginia. The western Virginia counties slightly favored Breckinridge, while the eastern counties threw their support just slightly more to Bell.[22]

And when Mr. Lincoln won, Virginians began focusing on the possibility of secession. In 1860, Virginia had more slaves (490,865) than any state in the United States.[23] The state was also in a very precarious geographical position, bordering Washington City and with great possibilities of being smack dab in the center of what could become the theater of fighting if a war ever came to fruition.

On January 7, 1861 in his message to the Virginia General Assembly, Governor John Letcher spoke about the secession of South Carolina and how that might affect Virginians. He said, "I have my convictions upon this question, and I give expression to them, in declaring my opposition at this time, to the call of a state convention. I see no necessity for it at this time, nor do I now see any good practical result that can be accomplished by it. I do not consider this a propitious time to moot the question, and I apprehend, from indications that have been exhibited, that serious difficulties and embarrassments will attend the

---

[22] http://www.virginiamemory.com/docs/1860_election_returns.pdf
[23] http://www.sonofthesouth.net/slavery/slave-maps/slave-census.htm

movement. Subsequent events may show the necessity for it. In 1833 and 1850, when the existence of the Union was seriously threatened, when the danger was imminent, the legislature accomplished everything desired, in a manner as satisfactory as it would have been accomplished, if the mode now suggested had been adopted. On neither occasion was the legislature chosen, with reference to the events which subsequently occurred, and which devolved upon them the necessity for such action as was taken, and which gave so much satisfaction to the people of Virginia and the whole country."[24]

The main focus early on was that Virginia needed to do anything and everything in its power to help avert a war. Virginia Judge John Robertson was sent to South Carolina with suggested propositions and constitutional amendments needed as compromise to maintain the peace. Virginia was proposing that the Crittenden resolutions be the basis for adjustments needed. As a peace commissioner, Robertson was treated very coldly. South Carolina maintained she had no interest in negotiating a peace.

The Charleston Mercury, the leading newspaper of the South, said of the Virginia proposals and its messenger: "Hear them if you please, treat them with civility, feed them and drench them with champagne. Let them go. Let us act as if they had never come; as if they had not spoken; as if they did not exist; and let them seem to preserve their treasury as it passed through some more supple agency than ours. The time has come when the voice of a Virginia politician, though he coos like a dove, should not be heard in the land of patriotic people."

When Robertson returned, the states of New York, Michigan, Ohio, Pennsylvania and Tennessee sent resolutions to Virginia saying, in effect, that those states did not condone Virginia's actions. Virginia's reaction to those resolutions from other states widened the gulf between the northern states and Virginia.

---

[24] http://docsouth.unc.edu/imls/vadel61/vadel61.html

Four candidates in 1860 election tearing the country apart
Source: *Harpers Weekly*

Chapter 12
Virginia ordinance of secession is defeated

In February, 1861, a convention was held at Mechanics Institute in Richmond, Virginia to discuss the possibility of secession. Delegates had been chosen by their individual counties, based on their political stand. Most of the delegates selected were pro-Union.

The topic was hotly contested for more than a month by the 152 convention delegates who leaned more toward a compromise than breaking with the Union. There was even hope that Virginia's actions in that regard might entice those states that had already left to return to the fold.

Southern states sent representatives to try to garner support to delay a vote they feared could be pro-Union.

The following incident showed how controversial being a delegate to the convention had been in certain areas of western Virginia. Reports from Barbour County Court House indicate a discussion was held in early 1861 to discuss succession from the Union. Spencer Dayton, the only man who spoke pro-Union, had a gun pointed at him. He fled out the courthouse window.

At a later meeting held at Martin Myer's Shoe Shop to choose delegates to the convention and aptly called the "Shoe Shop Convention" Dayton was elected as a delegate. Southern supporters gathered on the bridge to block Dayton's crossing in an attempt to keep him from his meeting in Wheeling. Dayton waited until late in the evening, in hopes that the bridge sentries would be sleeping. He encouraged his horse into a full gallop and sped across the bridge unharmed to get on his way to his important convention.

Jubal Early,[25] who later became a Confederate Civil War General, was one of the convention's staunchest Union supporters. Early insisted that "the enthusiasm for secession is

---

[25] http://www.jubalearly.org/jubal.html

short sighted, and likely to lead to war." Early, the Franklin County delegate, thought the voice of the southerners who did not own slaves (the majority of all southerners) were just as worthy of protection as the rights of those who do own slaves (the minority).

Jubal Early
Source: <u>americancivilwar.com</u>

Attorney John Baldwin from Staunton in the Shenandoah Valley, himself a slave owner, compared Virginia's place in the controversy to a lighthouse, and insisted that the state could withstand "the breasting and surging waves of Northern fanaticism and of Southern violence." He further thought that "the Lincoln administration does not represent an assault on Southern liberties, and even if it did, the U. S. Constitution protected them."

Western Virginian Waitman T. Willey who hailed from Morgantown, Virginia, reminded the delegates of the long standing disparity between the rights of the eastern Virginia slave owners and those in the westerners who tended to not have slaves.

The pro-secessionists brought protestors to the city to garner support for their side. Former Virginia Governor Henry Wise,[26] a radical secessionist, led the charge to delay the vote until they could strong-arm some more delegates.

---

[26] http://www.encyclopediavirginia.org/Wise_Henry_A_1806-1876

Henry Wise
Source: Library of Congress

When the vote was finally held on April 4, 1861, the ordinance of secession was soundly defeated by the vote of 90 to 45. When the vote was announced, staunch Whig John Jenney cheered. He insisted that "the secessionists are now without the slightest hope of success!"

On April 15, 1861, President Lincoln called on states to furnish 75,000 troops. Included in that quota were 2,340 requested from Virginia to be accepted at Gordonsville, Wheeling and Staunton.

Here is Virginia Governor John Letcher's response to the order.

Executive Department, Richmond, Va., April 15, 1861. Hon. Simon Cameron, Secretary of War:

SIR: I have received your telegram of the 15th, the genuineness of which I doubted. Since that time I have received your communications mailed the same day, in which I am requested to detach from the militia of the State of Virginia "the quota assigned in a table," which you append, "to serve as infantry or rifleman for the period of three months, unless sooner discharged." In reply to this communication, I have only to say that the militia of Virginia will not be furnished to the powers at Washington for any such use or purpose as they have in view.

Your object is to subjugate the Southern States, and a requisition made upon me for such an object - an object, in my judgment, not within the purview of the Constitution or the act of 1795 - will not be complied with.

You have chosen to inaugurate civil war, and, having done so, we will meet it in a spirit as determined as the administration has exhibited toward the South.

Respectfully, John Letcher[27]

John Letcher, Governor of Virginia
Source: civilwarscholars.com

---

[27] http://www.nytimes.com/1861/04/22/news/gov-letcher-s-proclamation-his-reply-secretary-cameron-state-affairs-norfolk.html

Chapter 13
Virginia votes again – this time to secede

When President Lincoln called up troops on April 15, the stance of many of the Virginia Convention delegates changed. They continued their discussions with the possibility of re-voting on the secession ordinance. Representatives of Mississippi, South Carolina and Georgia arrived at the convention and warned Virginians of the impending crisis. Virginians were reminded that the others thought Virginia would be in grave danger if she continued to side with the federal government.

Western Virginian Judge John J. Jackson predicted prior to the vote that "If the State of Virginia secedes from the Union, as sure as there is a God in Heaven, northwestern Virginia will secede from the State of Virginia!"[28]

Judge John J. Jackson   Source: West Virginia State Archives wvculture.org/history/statehood/statehood05.html

---

[28] http://www.wvhumanities.org/Statehood/kioskverbiage.pdf

On April 17, the convention voted again in secret session. In this instance, the ordinance of secession passed by the vote of 88 to 55.

Still, nearly a third of the elected delegates opposed secession even when it was clear that the secession crisis had become a civil war. Those in opposition included most of the delegates from the Ohio Valley counties and northwestern Virginia and a majority from the Shenandoah and Potomac River Valleys. The only eastern men to vote against secession on April 17 were one delegate from Henrico County, the delegate from Accomack County on the Eastern Shore, and the two delegates who represented Norfolk County and the city of Portsmouth.[29]

The delegates at that meeting who voted on the ordinance of secession from the western section and their recorded votes were as follows: Barbour (Samuel Woods, AYE), Berkeley (Allen C. Hammand, NAY; Edmund Pendleton, NAY), Braxton, Clay, Nicholas and Webster (Benjamin Wilson Byrne, NAY), Cabell (William McComas, NAY), Doddridge and Tyler (Chapman Johnson Stuart, NAY), Fayette and Raleigh (Henry L. Gillespie, AYE), Gilmer, Wirt & Calhoun (Currence Benjamin Conrad, NAY), Greenbrier (Samuel Price, NAY), Hampshire (Edward McCarty Armstrong, NAY; David Pugh, NAY), Hancock (George McCandless Porter, NAY), Harrison (John Snyder Carlile, NAY), Jackson and Roane (Franklin P. Turner, AYE), Jefferson (Logan Osburn, Sr., NAY), Kanawha (Spicer Patrick, NAY; George William Summers, NAY), Lewis County (Caleb Boggess, NAY), Logan, Boone and Wyoming (James Lawson, AYE), Marion (Ephraim Benoni Hall, NAY; Alpheus F. Haymond, NAY), Marshall (James Burley, NAY), Mason (James Henry Couch, NAY), Mercer (Napoleon B. French, AYE), Monongalia (Marshall Mortimer Dent, NAY; Waitman Thomas Whilley, NAY), Monroe (Allen Taylor Caperton, AYE; John Echols, AYE), Morgan (Johnson Orrick, AYE),

---

[29] www.virginiamemory.com/online_classroom/union_or_secession/unit/9/virginia_convention_votes_for_secession

Ohio (Sherrard Clemens, NAY; Chester Dorman Hubbard, NAY), Pendleton (Henry H. Masters, NAY), Pleasants and Ritchie (Cyrus Hall, AYE), Preston (William Guy Brown, NAY; James Clark McGrew, NAY), Putnam (James William Hoge, Sr. NAY), Randolph and Tucker (John H. Hughes, AYE), Taylor (John Sinsell Burdett, NAY), Tazewell, Buchanan and McDowell (William P. Cecil, AYE; Samuel Livingston Graham, AYE), Upshur (George W. Berlin, NAY), Wayne (Burwell Spurlock, NAY), Wetzel (Leonard Stout Hall, AYE), and Wood (John Jay Jackson, Sr., NAY).[30]

Several others were not delegates to the ordinance passage but were delegates either prior to or following the second secession vote – they included Jefferson County (Alfred Madison Barbour), Hardy County (Thomas Maslin), Harrison County (Benjamin Wilson) and Pocahontas County (Paul McNeel).[31]

Source: virginiamemory.com

---

[30] http://www.csawardept.com/documents/secession/VA/
[31] http://www.csawardept.com/documents/secession/VA/

Chapter 14

Westerners agree to form a new government

As soon as the Virginia secession ordinance passed, former Virginia Governor Henry A. Wise personally gave orders, of which Virginia Governor John Letcher was unaware, for the Virginia militia to seize the federal arsenal at Harpers Ferry and the navy yard at Portsmouth.[32]

At the secession vote, Wise brandished a revolver and pledged that "blood will be flowing at Harpers Ferry before night."[33]

It was ironic that Wise ordered the raid on the federal arsenal at Harpers Ferry. In 1859, when Wise was Governor of Virginia, John Brown and his band of men did that very same thing. Brown and six others were hanged for treason for their actions. Yet Wise received no such fate for attempting the very same mission.

The Virginia militia raided Harpers Ferry on April 18 in an attempt to secure the weapons and machinery from the gun factories. Troops garrisoned at the arsenal and commanded by 1st Lt. Robert Jones, Mounted Riflemen, set many of the buildings on fire to keep 15,000 arms stored there out of enemy hands. Then they fled the arsenal.[34]

---

[32] www.virginiamemory.com/online_classroom/union_or_secession/unit/9/southern_rights_convention

[33] www.encyclopediavirginia.org/Virginia_Constitutional_Convention_of_1861

[34] The War of Rebellion: The Official Records of the Union and Confederate Armies from www.simmonsgames.com/research/authors/USWarDept/ORA/OR-S1-V02-C009R.html#e1

The burning of Harpers Ferry arsenal
Source: *Harpers Weekly*

Much of the gun making equipment was taken from the arsenal to Richmond by the militia forces numbering in excess of 900 men who had made the assault. The event put the Harpers Ferry gun making operations out of business. They had manufactured over 600,000 firearms from 1804 until 1861. No gun was manufactured at Harpers Ferry after the April 18 raid.

The western Virginia delegation, led by John S. Carlisle of Clarksburg, walked out of the convention vowing at the time to form a new state government loyal to the Union. A number of the Union members of the convention from the western part of the State were threatened with personal violence on account of their opposition to the ordinance. They left Richmond and returned to their homes.

The secession ordinance was not binding until passed by the state's eligible voters. All white males over the age of 21 who had lived in the state at least two years were eligible to vote. On May 23, 1861 the ordinance of secession was voted on by the people all across the state of Virginia. The result was announced on June 25. The ordinance had passed with 132,201 voting in favor of secession and 37,451 against secession. Of the entire state's vote, western Virginians defeated the secession bill 29,983 to 14,937, though secession was favored by residents in 18 counties including Barbour, Boone, Braxton, Calhoun, Gilmer, Greenbrier, Hampshire, Hardy, Jefferson, Logan, McDowell, Mercer, Monroe, Pendleton, Raleigh, Tucker, Webster, and Wyoming.[35]

When Virginia voters approved the secession ordinance in May 1861, those in western Virginia who opposed leaving the Union had to decide whether to recreate a loyal Virginia government or to seek the creation of a new state. In practice, it proved necessary first to do the one and then the other.

County-by-county vote for the secession ordinance – showing counties now in West Virginia only – vote taken on May 23, 1861.[36]

County	For Secession	Against Secession
Barbour	857	626
Berkeley	508	1303
Boone	317	226
Braxton	553	114
Brooke	109	721
Cabell	232	882
Calhoun	279	81
Clay	102	102
Gilmer	338	186
Greenbrier	1016	110
Hampshire	1110	700
Hancock	23	743
Hardy	768	538
Harrison	614	1691
Jefferson	813	365
Kanawha	520	1697
Lewis	422	736

---

[35] http://www.newrivernotes.com/va/vasecesh.htm
[36] http://www.newrivernotes.com/va/vasecesh.htm

Logan	518	63
McDowell	196	17
Marshall	142	1993
Mason	119	1841
Mercer	871	67
Monroe	1189	79
Monongalia	110	2148
Ohio	157	3368
Pendleton	696	131
Pleasants	158	303
Preston	63	2256
Putnam	216	695
Raleigh	229	183
Tucker	106	54
Tyler	125	880
Upshur	306	701
Wayne	204	427
Webster	129	26
Wetzel	180	790
Wirt	150	507
Wood	257	1995
Wyoming	109	105
Total for West Virginia	14,937	29,983
Total for all of Virginia	114,260	32,606

Source: http://www.newrivernotes.com/va/vasecesh.htm

Chapter 15
Two Wheeling Conventions are held

Many western Virginians were quite upset with the secession vote as they favored the Union. But none was more excited than Archibald W. Campbell, editor of the *Wheeling Daily Intelligencer*. Campbell said the secession vote was a "mockery" of the wishes of the people and said the state was now in revolution. He said if the federal government didn't come to the aid of western Virginia, the western section of the state would be "delivered over to the despoilers and traitors, who in their wild fury are turning the eastern part of our State into a vast field of anarchy."

In his newspaper editorial, he called on western Virginia men to enroll with the Union army, calling on them to "summon every energy of your mind and heart and strength, and let the traitors who desecrate our borders see, and let history in all-time record it, that there was one green spot-one Swiss canton-one Scottish highland-one county of Kent-one province of Vendee, where unyielding patriotism rallied, and gathered, and stood, and won a noble triumph."[37]

Western Virginia leaders met in Clarksburg on April 22, 1861. With over 1,000 supporters outside the courthouse, resolutions were adopted to call a convention of the people to be held in Wheeling. Each county was asked to provide delegates to the meetings. Instead of denouncing secession, the men, after days of critical deliberation, decided instead that they would encourage people of western Virginia to vote against the ordinance of secession.

The First Wheeling Convention[38] was held May 13 to May 15, 1861. Among furious debate including deciding which of the 429 delegates who showed up should be seated, about all that was accomplished was to set up a way to elect

---

[37] *The Rendering of Virginia* by Granville D. Hall
[38] http://www.wvculture.org/history/statehood/statehood05.html

official delegates for the Second Wheeling Convention to be convened after the state's ordinance election. There was, however, an interesting development at the First Convention – that was Waitman T. Willey's insistence that John Carlile's proposal to create a new state was "triple treason – treason against the state of Virginia, the United States and the Confederacy."

Carlile's proposal included this enclosed drawing for the state of New Virginia.

Source: wvculture.org/history/statehood/statehood05.html

Additionally, the western Virginia leaders set up committees.

The ordinance election was held on May 23, and although it passed throughout the state by almost 100,000 votes, western Virginians defeated the secession bill 29,983 to 14,937.[39]

The Second Wheeling Convention[40] was held June 11 to June 25, 1861 at Washington Hall (now called the Custom House). Arthur Boreman was elected the convention chairman.

---

[39] http://www.newrivernotes.com/va/vasecesh.htm
[40] http://blueandgraytrail.com/event/Second_Wheeling_Convention

Each member of the convention, before taking his seat permanently, was required to take the following oath:

"I solemnly swear (or affirm,) that I will support the Constitution of the United States, and the laws made in pursuance thereof, as the supreme law of the land, anything in the Constitution and laws of the State of Virginia, or in the Ordinances of the Convention which assembled at Richmond on the 13th of February, 1861, to the contrary notwithstanding; and that I will uphold and defend the Government of Virginia as vindicated and restored by the Convention which assembled at Wheeling, on the 11th day of June, 1861."

Eighty-seven delegates from 32 counties were seated. All the members except one took the oath. The one who wasn't seated left to go to Richmond.

Convention at Wheeling's Custom House
Source: *Harpers Weekly* July 4, 1861 issue

Chapter 16
The new government applies for statehood

The Second Wheeling Convention continued the discussions. The longer they debated the issues, the less they accomplished. The main issue was the decision to either form a reorganized government or to form a new state. The first was much easier to accomplish than the latter.

On June 13, John Carlile proposed what he called "A Declaration of the People of Virginia"[41] which called for the reorganization of the existing government of Virginia. The experienced delegate called the differences from the eastern and western Virginia "irreconcilable." He reminded his fellow delegates that the western section of Virginia had been discriminated against since the original Virginia constitution in 1776. Although the delegates finally agreed to separate from Virginia, they were not as agreeable on how to accomplish that goal.

By June 20, the convention delegates finally agreed to a compromise, forming the Restored or Reorganized Government of Virginia. Francis H. Pierpont from Marion County was elected as the governor. The new government was to become effective on July 1, 1861. The government was to become the loyalist, Union government for Virginia. It was believed that national offices, vacated due to the secession of Virginia, might be available to the newly formed government.

For those who preferred to create a new state, the crux of the problem was how to satisfy the U. S. Constitutional process for creation of a state from the boundaries of an existing state. Leaders such as John S. Carlile and Francis H. Pierpont influenced the Second Wheeling Convention to form a Restored or Reorganized Government of Virginia[42] with headquarters in Wheeling. This government provided a loyal,

---

[41] http://www.wvculture.org/history/statehood/declaration.html
[42] http://www.wvculture.org/history/statehoo.html

Unionist government for Virginia and eventually provided the necessary consent to the creation of West Virginia.

The Restored or Reorganized Government immediately set about the task of re-establishing government functions at the state, county, and local level. Virginia's secession had split local officials into Union and Confederate factions. These men fought one another for control of county and local governmental units, resulting in anarchy in much of western Virginia. Pierpont, elected governor of the Restored or Reorganized Government of Virginia on June 20, 1861, called on President Abraham Lincoln for military aid. Gen. George B. McClellan and his army brought security to Pierpont's government and legitimacy when McClellan recognized him as the Governor of Virginia. Pierpont called the newly elected legislature into session on July 1. The General Assembly immediately began the re-establishment of governmental functions, provided for the raising of military units for federal service, and elected new U. S. Senators and members of the House of Representatives to represent Virginia in Washington.

Francis Pierpont
Source: West Virginia State Archives
<u>wvculture.org</u>

The Restored or Reorganized Government of Virginia set up shop at all levels of government including local, state and county government. In the beginning stages, the conflict between Union and Confederate leanings caused quite a bit of confusion throughout western Virginia as men fought for political power.

On June 20, Governor Francis H. Pierpont, requested military aid from President Abraham Lincoln. Here is the telegram he wrote:

Commonwealth of Virginia, Executive Dept., Wheeling, June 21, 1861

To His Excellency the President of the United States:

SIR: Reliable information has been received at this department from various parts of the State that large numbers of evil-minded persons have banded together in military organizations with intent to overthrow the Government of the State; and for that purpose have called to their aid like-minded persons from other States, who, in pursuance of such call, have invaded this Commonwealth. They are now making war on the loyal people of the State. They are pressing citizens against their consent into their military organization, and seizing and appropriating their property to aid in the rebellion.

I have not at my command sufficient military force to suppress this rebellion and violence. The Legislature cannot be convened in time to act in the premises; it therefore becomes my duty as Governor of this Commonwealth to call on the Government of the United States for aid to repress such rebellion and violence.

I therefore earnestly request that you will furnish a military force to aid in suppressing the rebellion, and to protect the good people of this Commonwealth from domestic violence.

I have the honor to be, with great respect, your obedient servant.

(Signed,) F.H. Pierpont, Governor

At the same time, Pierpont made official application for recognition of the newly formed state from President Lincoln and Congress. He enclosed the following map.

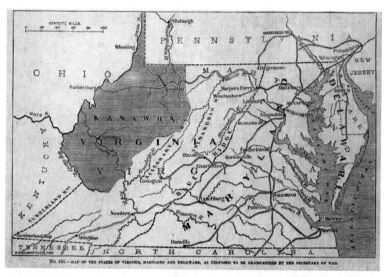

The area of western Virginia was known originally as Kanawha. The eastern panhandle counties were not added until later.
Source: wvculture.org

Chapter 17

Statehood try is sanctioned in Washington

The following letter was received from President Lincoln, as written by the Secretary of War:

War Department, Washington, June 25, 1861

Hon. Francis H. Pierpont, Governor Commonwealth of Virginia, Wheeling, Va.

SIR: In reply to your application of the 21st instant, for the aid of the Federal Government to repel from Virginia the lawless invaders now perpetrating every species of outrage upon, persons and property, throughout a large portion of the State, the President directs me to say that a large additional force will soon be sent to your relief.

The President, however, never supposed that a brave and free people, though surprised and unarmed could long be subjected by a class of political adventures always adverse to them; and the fact that they have already rallied, reorganized their government, and checked the march of these invaders, demonstrates how justly he appreciated them.

The failure, hitherto, of the State authorities, in consequence of the circumstances to which I have adverted, to organize its quota of troops called for by the President, imposed upon him the necessity of providing himself for their organization; and this has been done to some extent. But instructions have now been given to the agents of the Federal Government to proceed hereafter under your direction, and the company and field officers will be commissioned by you.

I have the honor to be, very respectfully,

Your obedient servant,

(Signed) Simon Cameron, Secretary of War.

Not only would the new government be receiving much needed military aid, but the federal government had also informally recognized the new state government.

The Lincoln administration urged Secretary of War Simon Cameron to "Please lose no time, in giving an interview to Adjt. Genl. Wheat of Western Virginia, and furnish him, if possible with what arms, equipage &c. he needs. This is very important, and should not be neglected or delayed." That memo was followed up by another that called for the government "to furnish 5,000 stands of arms to the state government at Wheeling" if it could be done "without endangering other points too much."

On July 1, the new state legislature would be called into session. The legislature also set up a constitutional convention for the fall. Delegates were to be elected on October 24, 1861 to write that new state constitution.

Article IV, Section 3 of the U.S. Constitution had set the parameters for the formation of a new state. It is clear and concise, saying "new states may be admitted by the Congress into this Union; but no new state shall be formed or erected within the Jurisdiction of any other State; nor any state be formed by the Junction of two or more States, or Parts of States, without the consent of the Legislatures of the States concerned as well as of the Congress."

That was certainly a concern for the new government.

Simon Cameron, Secretary of War
Source: Library of Congress

Chapter 18
A Constitutional Convention is proposed

The ongoing war and the political upheaval caused by the secession of Virginia and the formation of the Restored or Reorganized Government of Virginia were already causing additional problems between the eastern and western sections.

Recently, Virginia had stopped work on the Trans-Allegheny Lunatic Asylum in Weston in Lewis County in western Virginia. At the same time, they cancelled a loan for West Liberty Academy in Ohio County. This troubled the new legislature seated in Wheeling. Both of those counties were loyal to the new government. The new government reacted by seizing $27,000 in gold from the Weston Bank belonging to the commonwealth of Virginia that was to fund the projects.[43]

In the July legislative session of the new government, the delegates elected John S. Carlile and Waitman T. Willey to replace U. S. Senators R. M. T. Hunter and James M. Mason, Virginia Senators who had resigned when Virginia seceded. The two new Senators were appointed to fill those vacated seats. Kellian V. Whaley, William G. Brown and Jacob B. Blair were elected as members of the House of Representatives to the 37th Congress.

Congress re-confirmed the recognition of the Restored and Reorganized Government of Wheeling, Virginia as the House of Representatives accepted the new members on July 4. Nine days later the new U. S. Senators were also officially received.

In President Abraham Lincoln's message to Congress, delivered on July 4, the president said "the people of Virginia have thus allowed this giant insurrection to make its nest within her borders; and this government has no choice left but to deal with it, where it finds it. And it has the less regret, as

---

[43] http://trans-alleghenylunaticasylum.com/main/history5.html

the loyal citizens have, in due form, claimed its protection. These loyal citizens and this government is bound to recognize and protect as being Virginia."

The Second Wheeling Convention met again on August 6, 1861, following a six-week adjournment. Amongst the pressing business of the delegates was the distancing of themselves from the former state of Virginia, both symbolically and legally. They voted to render null and void every resolution approved by the Virginian Secession Convention. And then they took on the statehood debate in earnest.

While many delegates were unsure of the proper path to take, John Carlile was not among them. He told his colleagues that they needed to "Cut the knot now!" He argued that regardless of the outcome of the war, western Virginia needed to take care of its future. He reminded them that eastern Virginia had always treated the western counties with disdain and had discriminated against them for as far back as the founding of the country in 1776.

Although still unable to reach agreement on many issues facing the convention, the delegates agreed that whatever action was taken, including the writing of a new constitution, would have to be sent to the voters for ratification. The creation of a new state remained a central issue. They decided to authorize a Constitutional Convention, to which delegates would be elected on October 24, 1861.

Crowd outside Custom's House in Wheeling
Frank Leslie's Illustrated, August 10, 1861 issue
Source: printsoldandrare.com

Chapter 19
Attorney General Bates calls movement legal

The federal government's policies continued to favor the newly formed government. In August, 1861, when the president made trade with the rebel states illegal, he exempted those parts of the Virginia lying west of the Allegheny Mountains.

That same month, Attorney General Edward Bates gave his legal opinion on the formation of the Restored or Reorganized Government of Virginia. He wrote that he "rejoiced in the movement in western Virginia, as a legal, constitutional and safe refuge from revolution and anarchy -- as at once an example and fit instrument for the restoration of all the revolted States."

In the August, 1861, delegates from the Second Wheeling Convention discussed where the final boundaries of the new state would be. Following the debate, the convention added Pocahontas, Greenbrier, Monroe, Mercer, and McDowell Counties. Additionally, they were willing to add others, namely Jefferson, Berkeley, Frederick, Morgan, Hampshire, Hardy, and Pendleton Counties, if the citizens in those counties favored statehood. Every county except Frederick County voted to join the new state. There were, however, concerns as to the legitimacy of the vote in some of those eastern counties. (Note -- Mineral, Grant, Lincoln, Summers, Mingo, Morgan, Jefferson and Berkeley counties were formed after statehood was official.)

In the fall of 1861, arms and ammunition started arriving in western Virginia from the federal government. Their support of western Virginia was penned in the diary of President Lincoln's secretary John Hay who wrote "Loyalty will be safer in western Virginia than rebellion will be on the eastern slopes of the Blue Ridge."

Major General George McClellan, Commander of the Department of Ohio, realized the importance of the pro-Union people of western Virginia saying, "We have in our power to unite that people firmly to us forever. I hope the opportunity may not be permitted to pass by."

Secretary of War Simon Cameron supported his general's position saying "it is deemed highly important that the Union men in western Virginia be aided and encouraged in every way possible, and it is desired that you and those under your command should do so as far as you can."

But even with General McClellan's support and encouragement, the new state had trouble recruiting Union soldiers for the cause. General McClellan had said previously that he was certain a "very considerable number of volunteers can be raised in western Virginia." But he was finding out that he had perhaps been too optimistic.

In August, the *Wellsburg Herald* newspaper, took the new state to task in an editorial, critical of its inability to recruit soldiers for the Union army. The newspaper editor said "a pretty condition Northwestern Virginia is in to establish herself as a separate state...after all the drumming and all the gas about a separate state she has actually organized in the field four not entire regiments of soldiers and one of these hails almost entirely from the Panhandle."

Western Virginia's pro-Union sentiment and strategic location gave significant advantages to the Union. The Baltimore and Ohio Railroad, critical to transporting the Union supplies, crossed over two hundred miles through fourteen western Virginia counties. The Ohio River, the western boundary of western Virginia, was important for transportation. Western Virginia's addition to the Union was also symbolically important as a Border State.

Baltimore and Ohio Railroad in Virginia
(today West Virginia)
Source: eduborail.org

Chapter 20
Voters unanimously approve statehood

The voters of the new state cast a favorable vote on October 24, 1861 supporting the statehood measure by a wide margin – 19,189 in favor and only 781 opposed. But even with that apparent overwhelming support, the vote was not without controversy. The 1860 election showed 65,634 eligible voters in the 48 counties, yet only 30 percent voted in this important election. In several counties less than ten percent of the voters cast a ballot. And over 70 percent of the "aye" votes came from just 16 counties. Another thirteen counties provided no vote at all. In one area, it was reported that Ohio soldiers had cast votes.[44]

Legislator Chapman J. Stuart of Wheeling was troubled by the turnout. He told his compatriots, "to look at the figures to satisfy the mind of every member that even a majority of the people within the thirty-nine counties have never come to the polls and expressed their sentiments in favor of the new state. In a voting population of some 40,000 to 50,000, we see a poll of only 17,627 and even some of them were in the army." (Stuart's population estimates came from just the original 39 counties.)

The First Constitutional Convention convened on November 26, 1861 to write the new constitution. One of their biggest concerns was the slavery issue. The representatives knew they needed a compromise position because Congress was not going to allow a pro-slavery state into the Union.

After much consideration, a proposal by Reverend Gordon Battle of Ohio County was accepted that simply stated, "No slave shall be brought, or free person of color be permitted to come into this State for permanent residence."

On December 3, 1861, a rather interesting discussion took place in the First Constitutional Convention concerning

---

[44] civilwartalk.org

the naming of the new state. The name "West Virginia" was adopted, but not by unanimous vote. Thirty voted for "West Virginia" including John Hall (Convention President), and delegates Brumfield, Caldwell, Carskadon, Cassady, Dille, Dolly, Hansley, Raymond, Hubbs, Hervey, Hagar, Irvine, Lauck, Mahon, O'Brien, Parsons, Parker, Sinsel, Simmons, B. F. Stewart, C. J. Stuart, Sheets, Soper, Taylor, Trainer, Willey, Walker, Warder, and Wilson.

Nine voted for "Kanawha," including delegates Brown of Kanawha, Battelle, Chapman, Harrison, Lamb, Montague, Paxton, Ruffner, and Van Winkle. Two, Brooks and Powell, cast votes for "Western Virginia." Two others, Pomeroy and Stevenson of Wood County, voted for "Allegheny." Mr. Brown of Preston County voted for the name "Augusta."[45]

Recording of the vote to name the new state
Source: wvculture.org/history/statehood/statename.html

On February 18, 1862, the new state constitution was unanimously approved by the delegates to the Constitutional Convention. It was then submitted to the voters for their approval. The citizens voted 18,862 to 514 in favor of the new constitution.

The convention adjourned for its final time on February 20, 1862. U. S. Senator John Carlile was to propose the statehood bills in Washington where it was hoped they would receive quick approval from Congress and President Abraham Lincoln.

---

[45] http://www.wvculture.org/history/statehood/statename.html

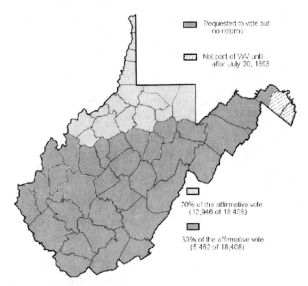

Map showing popular vote on the statehood issue
Source: civilwartalk.com

Chapter 21

A new split occurs north to south

Even with the statehood bill being sent to Congress and with the state's overwhelming vote, there were factions that were "jumping ship" on the statehood issue. Some who had thought the idea excellent at first were having second thoughts. And this time the split wasn't between the eastern Virginians and the western Virginians, but rather between those who lived in the northern part of the new region and those living in the south.

Southern interests were different. Some were selling salt, which was an important product to the Confederates. Some didn't favor joining as a free state in regards to the slavery issue. Others were infuriated that their northern neighbors would not support a state funded railroad in their area, the Kanawha Valley.

When a suggestion to emancipate the slaves came to the floor of the Constitutional Convention in Wheeling, delegates from Harrison County south to the Kentucky line threatened to walk out of the meetings. Others were just as strong in the opposite direction, believing that they couldn't support statehood if slavery were not totally abolished. The convention instead passed a gradual emancipation bill that got the majority vote but was not something that either side was too supportive of. As we will see, Congress had its own ideas on the status of slavery in the new state thereby negating the compromise reached at the convention.

The Confederate army, led by Thomas J. "Stonewall" Jackson who had grown up in western Virginia, continued to wreck the Baltimore and Ohio Railroad especially in the eastern panhandle. Jackson's men blew up the Harpers Ferry bridge and stole and/or destroyed Baltimore and Ohio Railroad equipment in Martinsburg in June of 1861. Those destructive influences angered many western Virginians and helped bring even more support to the formation of a new separate state.

In the Lincoln Cabinet, Simon Cameron favored the Pennsylvania Railroad over the Baltimore and Ohio Railroad and therefore was not supportive of statehood. When Edwin Stanton, a staunch Baltimore and Ohio Railroad supporter took Cameron's place, the fortunes of the new state got a boost. Stanton was well known by many pro-statehood delegates in western Virginia. And by adding the eastern panhandle counties to the new state boundaries upon their county approval, the Baltimore and Ohio Railroad properties would be extricated completely from Virginia and could operate entirely in the North.

Two other factors played into the statehood efforts. A serious Union loss in the battle of Fredericksburg in December, 1862, and the mid-term election defeat of many Republicans left President Lincoln with little option when it came to deciding how to vote on statehood. The radicals in Congress, usually not supporting anything Mr. Lincoln wanted, threw their support behind statehood as a way to reduce Virginia's influence on all fronts by taking away one-third of the commonwealth's territory. By favoring statehood, they were able to accomplish in Congress the victory that seemed to have been eluding them on the battlefield.

"Stonewall" Jackson stealing the Baltimore and
Ohio Railroad equipment at Martinsburg
Source: Mort Künstler artist

64

Chapter 22

Statehood bill approved by U.S. Congress

The United States Constitution had set the parameters for the formation of a new state quite clearly and distinctly in Article IV, Section 3 – "A new state may be admitted by the Congress into this Union; but no new state shall be formed or erected within the Jurisdiction of any other state; nor any state formed by the Junction of two or more States, of parts of States, without the Consent of the Legislatures of the states concerned as well as of the Congress."

The original state of Virginia, now a part of the Confederate States of America, was never going to grant permission for 1/3 of its original land mass to break off and become a new state. They had not supported much of anything regarding their western brethren in the entire history of the state going back all the way to 1776. That being said, on May 13, 1862, the Restored or Reorganized Government of Virginia granted itself permission to form a new state. That pronouncement remains as controversial today as it was the day it was announced. And many argue as a result of that, the state of West Virginia was formed illegally.

When the statehood bills were introduced in Congress, they did not pass along as smoothly as the new state's representatives had hoped. Massachusetts Senator Charles Sumner, the famed anti-slavery politician who had been nearly beaten to death in the U. S. Senate in 1856, demanded the new state constitution free all of their slaves. He feared the addition of a slave state into the Union. Western Virginia Senator John Carlile insisted that only another statewide election could settle the slavery issue.

SOUTHERN CHIVALRY — ARGUMENT versus CLUB'S.

Preston Brooks attacking Charles Sumner in the
chamber of the U.S Senate – 1856
Source: historyconfidential.com

Carlile's colleague in the U. S. Senate, Waitman Willey, proposed an amendment (dubbed the Willey Amendment) calling for "the children of slaves born within the limits of this state after the fourth day of July, eighteen hundred and sixty-three, shall be free; and all slaves within the said state who shall, at the time aforesaid, be under the age of ten years, shall be free when they arrive at the age of twenty-one years; and all slaves over ten and under twenty-one years, shall be free when they arrive at the age of twenty-five years; and no slave shall be permitted to come into the state for permanent residence therein." The U. S. Senate approved the statehood bill on July 14, 1862 that contained the Willey Amendment. The vote was twenty-three for and seventeen against with eight abstentions.

Senator Carlile voted against the statehood bill, causing him to be seen as a traitor back home in western Virginia. When he returned home, he was never elected again to any office in his home state, though it could be argued that the state would have never been formed without his diligent leadership.

It took the U. S. House of Representatives a much longer time to come to grips with the statehood bill. They did not approve it until December 10, 1862 by a vote of ninety-six for and fifty-five against.[46]

U.S. Senator John Carlile
Source – wvculture.org

[46] http://www.umaine.edu/khronikos/docs/papers/archive/hodges.pdf

Chapter 23
President Lincoln signs the statehood bill

With Congressional approval coming on the statehood bill for West Virginia, by the U.S. Senate on July 14, 1862 and by the U. S. House of Representatives on December 10, 1862, the bill had one step remaining in Washington. It needed President Abraham Lincoln's signature. If the president didn't deal with the bill within ten days, it would automatically become law.

President Lincoln's long-time friend from Illinois, Senator Orville Browning delivered the bill to him. Browning noted at the time that his friend "was distressed at its passage." Its passage was thought to be a sign of Lincoln's failure to attempt reconstruction in Virginia.

The president looked for support among his Cabinet members, but found very little. He asked them to submit comments about the impending statehood. Secretary of the Navy Gideon Welles was emphatic in his opposition saying "this is not the time to divide the old Commonwealth. The requirements of the Constitution are not complied with, as they in good faith should be."

Attorney General Edward Bates and Postmaster General Montgomery Blair joined Welles in opposing the bill. Bates' opposition was certainly interesting since in August he had called the statehood movement both legal and constitutional. At this point in time, he told the president, "I give it as my opinion that the bill in question is unconstitutional; and also, by its own intrinsic demerits, highly inexpedient. And I persuade myself that Congress, upon maturer thought, will be glad to be relieved by a veto, from the evil consequences of such improvident legislation."

Secretary of State William Seward, Secretary of the Treasury Salmon Chase, and Secretary of War Edwin Stanton offered their support.[47]

---

[47] http://www.as.wvu.edu/wvhistory/documents/037.pdf

Mr. Lincoln certainly realized the implications of the new state. He needed their pro-Union support but was not sure that they could support him with any great help militarily. He was also treading gingerly in regard to the other Border States. He was criticized mightily for allowing West Virginia's secession from Virginia when at the same time he opposed secession of the other states. His response was "it is said that the admission of West Virginia, is secession, and tolerated only because it is our secession. Well, if we call it by that name, there is still difference enough between secession against the Constitution, and secession in favor of the Constitution."

On the last possible day, December 31, 1862, President Lincoln wrote his "Opinion on the Admission of West Virginia in the Union" [48] saying the government could "scarcely dispense with the aid of West Virginia in this struggle; much less can we afford to have her against us, in Congress and in the field. Her brave and good men regard her admission into the Union as a matter of life and death....Again, the admission of the new State turns that much slave soil to free; and thus, is certain and irrevocable encroachment upon the cause of the rebellion."

And with that said, he signed the West Virginia statehood bill.

The very next day, January 1, 1863, President Abraham Lincoln announced his Emancipation Proclamation, freeing the slaves in the states of rebellion. One paragraph of that document is of particular note. The document exempted the forty-eight counties designated as West Virginia. [49]

Statehood for West Virginia was one giant step away from reality. It would still take a majority vote from the citizens of West Virginia to approve the statehood bill. That election was set for March 26, 1863.

---

[48] http://www.wvculture.org/history/statehood/lincolnopinion.html
[49] http://www.nps.gov/ncro/anti/emancipation.html

President Abraham Lincoln and West Virginia Statehood
Source: <u>abrahamlincolnclassroom.org</u>

Chapter 24
Voters unanimously approve the bill

The West Virginia Constitutional Convention was called back into session in February, 1863. They unanimously approved the Willey Amendment into their constitution calling for "the children of slaves born within the limits of this state after the fourth day of July, eighteen hundred and sixty-three, shall be free; and all slaves within the said state who shall, at the time aforesaid, be under the age of ten years, shall be free when they arrive at the age of twenty-one years; and all slaves over ten and under twenty-one years, shall be free when they arrive at the age of twenty-five years; and no slave shall be permitted to come into the state for permanent residence therein."

The statehood bill including the Willey Amendment was submitted to the voters of West Virginia for ratification. The bill passed by a landslide, 27,749 for ratification and 572 opposed.

On April 20, President Lincoln issued the following proclamation:

"Whereas, by the Act of Congress approved the 31st day of December, last, the State of West Virginia was declared to be one of the United States of America, and was admitted into the Union on an equal footing with the original States in all respects whatever, upon the condition that certain changes should be duly made in the proposed Constitution for that State;

And, whereas, proof of a compliance with that condition as required by the Second Section of the Act aforesaid, has been submitted to me;

Now, therefore, be it known, that I, Abraham Lincoln, President of the United States, do, hereby, in pursuance of the Act of Congress aforesaid, declare and proclaim that the said act shall take effect and be in force, from and after sixty days from the date hereof.

In witness whereof, I have here unto set my hand and caused the Seal of the United States to be affixed.

Sixty days later, on June 20, 1863, in accordance with the terms of this proclamation. West Virginia entered the Union. As stated in the beginning of this paper, it was the 35th state of the nation, and the first one to enter during the administration of President Lincoln.

(Signed) Abraham Lincoln, President[50]

In May, Arthur I. Boreman was placed in nomination by the Constitutional Union party of West Virginia to run as governor. No other candidate was nominated. Thus Boreman became the first Governor of West Virginia. Francis Pierpont, who had been Governor of the Restored and Reorganized Government of Virginia, continued as governor moving to Alexandria and controlling Union held portions of Virginia. Pierpont also ordered residents in Jefferson and Berkeley Counties to be allowed to vote for admission into West Virginia. With Union troops placed outside the polling places, both counties voted for inclusion into the new state of West Virginia. That vote also remains controversial even to today.

---

[50] http://www.wvculture.org/history/journal_wvh/wvh24-4.html

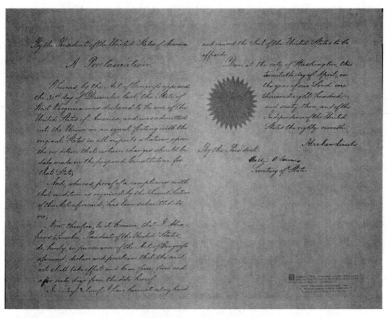

President Lincoln's statehood proclamation of April 20, 1863
Source: omninternet.com

Chapter 25

West Virginia becomes the 35th state

One hundred fifty years ago, on June 20, 1863, West Virginia became the 35th state of the United States.

In his remarks on that day, West Virginia's first Governor, Arthur I. Boreman, reminded the citizens of the long and hard road that they had been down to finally be recognized and treated with the "same rights and immunities as, and upon equal footing with, the other States of the Union."

Governor Boreman said "West Virginia should long since have had a separate State existence. The East has always looked upon that portion of the State west of the mountains, as a sort of outside appendage – a territory in a state of pupilage. The unfairness and inequality of legislation is manifest on every page of the statute book; they had an unjust majority in the Legislature by the original Constitution of the State, and have clung to it with the utmost tenacity ever since; they have collected heavy taxes from us, and have spent large sums in the construction of railroads and canals in the East, but have withheld appropriations from the West; they have refused to make any of the modern improvements by which trade and travel could be carried on from the one section to the other, thus treating us as strangers; our people could not get to the Capital of their State by any of the usual modes of traveling, without going through the State of Maryland and the District of Columbia. The East and the West have always been two peoples."

Governor Boreman continued by saying "our State is the child of the rebellion; yet our peace, prosperity and happiness, and, not only ours, but that of the whole country, depends on the speedy suppression of this attempt to overthrow the Government of our fathers; and it is my duty, as soon as these ceremonies are closed, to proceed at once to aid the Federal authorities in their efforts to stay its destructive hand."[51]

Granville D. Hall, a stenographer who had recorded in short-hand all the proceedings of the struggle for West Virginia statehood as a reporter for the *Wheeling Daily Intelligencer*, said of the final outcome: "the dream of generations had 'come true.' Some whose hopes and labors had been crowned were not here to enjoy the fruition. At last we had come to the end of the toilsome road; the close of the fierce, the bitter, the enduring struggle; had triumphed over perils by land and sea, by flood and field-the assaults of open, the snares of secret foes, the timidity of the faint-hearted, the rashness of the bold. At last we were out of the wilderness; not only in sight but in possession of the Promised Land. The past, with its anxieties and bitterness, was to be forgotten save for its lessons of wisdom and patience; and now all faces turned to the future, rosy in the dawn of enfranchisement and progress!"[52]

Date stone of the official formation of the new state of West Virginia on the grounds of the Jefferson County Courthouse, Charles Town, WV   Source: Author photo

---

[51] http://www.wvculture.org/history/boremania.html
[52] *The Rendering of Virginia* by Granville D. Hall

Chapter 26
Legality of statehood still debated

The statehood of West Virginia became official on June 20, 1863 – 150 years ago. The formation of the new state had been controversial from day one. It remains so to this day.

Even Confederate President Jefferson Davis weighed in on the issue saying, "the subsequent organization of the State of West Virginia and its separation from the State of Virginia were acts of secession. Thus we have, in their movements, insurrection, revolution, and secession. . . . To admit a state under such a government is entirely unauthorized, revolutionary, subversive of the Constitution and destruction of the Union of States."

Some historians and lawyers have contended that the state of West Virginia was formed illegally. The Supreme Court finally got to resolve a portion of the controversy in the case *Virginia vs. West Virginia* which was filed by the Virginia General Assembly.

The Virginia legislature had several gripes concerning the inclusion into the state of West Virginia of the counties of Berkeley and Jefferson, located in the eastern panhandle. On May 23, 1863, Berkeley County's citizens had ratified their entrance into West Virginia (certified on August 5). On September 14 that same year, Jefferson County also voted to join West Virginia (made official on November 2).[53]

Virginia sued, contending that U. S. Congress had given its consent to the splitting off of those two counties to West Virginia in March 1866 when the Commonwealth of Virginia had already withdrawn its consent.

The Supreme Court's split decision (6-3) was rendered on March 7, 1871. The highest court in the land ruled on Virginia's complaint, saying that since both the President and

---

[53] www.mindserpent.com/American_History/federal/military/lin_wv.html

Congress recognized the Restored and Reorganized Government of Virginia as the official government of Virginia at the time, the entire process was therefore legal. The majority opinion of the high court said, "although the elections had been postponed due to a 'hostile' environment, the majority concluded that the Reorganized Government of Virginia had acted in 'good faith' to carry out its electoral duties in the two counties."

At the same time, the minority opinion stated that by the time Congress gave its consent (on March 10, 1866), the legislature of Virginia had already withdrawn its consent to the transfer of the two counties. Therefore the action was illegal.

What the Supreme Court did not rule on was the constitutionality of the state's formation. That had not been a part of the lawsuit.

According to the U. S. Constitution, "new States may be admitted by the Congress into this Union; but no new States shall be formed or erected within the Jurisdiction of any other State; nor any State be formed by the Junction of two or more States, or parts of States, without the Consent of the Legislatures of the States concerned as well as of the Congress."

In the case of West Virginia's statehood, since Virginia was no longer part of the Union, the new Restored and Reorganized Government of Virginia granted itself permission to organize the western sector into its own state.

West Virginia flag
Source: officialbridgeday.com

Chapter 27
The aftermath of statehood

From June of 1861 through April of 1865, the state of Virginia had two governments operating simultaneously. One was the government in Richmond, Virginia that was part of the Confederate States of America. The other had its center in Wheeling, Virginia and operated first as the Restored and Reorganized Government of Virginia and then as of June 20, 1863, as the new state of West Virginia. At that time, the Restored and Reorganized Government of Virginia moved its headquarters to Alexandria, where Frances Pierpont continued as governor.[54]

The great seal of the new state was commissioned by the state legislature. It was designed by a Doddridge County man, Joseph H. Diss Debar. The seal contains the Latin inscription *"Montani Semper Liberi"* which translates to "Mountaineers Are Always Free." It was officially adopted on September 26, 1863.[55]

One of the repercussions of the Civil War to those who favored the south took place in 1865 and 1866 when West Virginia's legislature, which at the time was governed by Republicans, passed the Voter's Oath Law and the Voter Registration Law. The laws prohibited anyone who could not prove their loyalty to the Union and to West Virginia from voting, holding public office, teaching, or filing suit. The laws rather effectively kept the former Confederate supporters (mostly Democrats) at bay.[56] By 1871, those laws that had affected as many as 20,000 West Virginians had been rescinded.

---

[54] http://www.virginiamemory.com/online_classroom/union_or_secession/unit/11/restored_government_of_virginia
[55] http://www.wvencyclopedia.org/articles/614
[56] http://www.legis.state.wv.us/Educational/Kids_Page/5.html

In 1872, the original state constitution was rewritten at a Constitutional Convention and ratified by the people. That 1872 state constitution is still in place today, although there have been 70 amendments approved over the years.

The state capital of West Virginia today is located in the city of Charleston, in Kanawha County. But that hasn't always been true. From 1863 to 1870 the capital was in Wheeling. From 1870 to 1875 it was moved to Charleston. From 1875 to 1885 it was moved back to Wheeling. And it has been in Charleston every year since 1885.

West Virginia Day, June 20, has been celebrated every year since 1927. That was the year the West Virginia legislature formally recognized it as a state holiday.

Although West Virginia's state constitution provided for payment to the Commonwealth of Virginia for infrastructure improvements, it took a Supreme Court ruling in 1915 before West Virginia finally was required to start paying on the balance of about $12 million still owed. The final payment was not made until 1939.

The two states have continued to clash over boundaries in the Harpers Ferry area, between Loudoun County, Virginia and Jefferson County, West Virginia. A boundary commission was established by each state in 1991 to look at the 15 miles in question.

As recently as a few years ago, there was talk of the eastern panhandle counties of Morgan, Berkeley and Jefferson Counties returning to Virginia due to their perception that the government in Charleston was ignoring them.

Seal of West Virginia
Source – www.wv.gov

Part II
Important participants in the process leading to West Virginia Statehood
(Listed alphabetically)

Chapter 1
Arthur I. Boreman

Arthur Ingraham Boreman, the man West Virginians had chosen as their first governor, was born in Waynesburg, Pennsylvania in 1823. His family moved to Middlebourne, Tyler County in western Virginia when he was four years old. He studied law and passed the Virginia bar in 1845. He moved to Parkersburg around that time and lived there the remainder of his life.

Boreman had been a very active political leader for many years. He had been a member of the Virginia General Assembly from 1855 until the state seceded from the Union in 1861.

He was the president of the Second Wheeling Convention in 1861 which established the Restored and Reorganized Government of Virginia. He served that new government as a circuit court judge. Boreman also worked with other western Virginia leaders to secure the statehood bill that was eventually passed by Congress and signed by President Lincoln.

Boreman was 40 years old when he was chosen to govern the new state. He ended up serving as West Virginia's Governor from 1863 to 1869. While governor, he worked judiciously to develop public schools in West Virginia. He pushed to establish the West Virginia Code and the Board of Public Works. During the Civil War, he sent militia units to help fend off Confederate forces in the southern reaches of the state.

He also helped established the voter's test law that denied the right to vote, hold office, practice law, teach or sue to anyone who could not prove their loyalty to the Union.

In 1869, Boreman was elected to the U.S. Senate where he served until 1875. In 1888, he was elected as a circuit court judge. He died in 1896.

His obituary paints an amazing portrait of the state's first governor saying "there were none, seemingly, who possessed that untiring energy, sleepless industry and indomitable will, peculiar to him, and which were in that crisis essential to safe and successful leadership. He had the grit that men admire. His backbone was as stiff as the Bunker Hill monument. He believed he was right in standing by the flag. His position was the Unity of the Nation; and there he stood as firmly as the eternal rocks that based the hills around him. The people saw that there were in his make-up those essentials that mark the leadership of men, so they called him to the front and placed him upon the pedestal of commanding position." The statement goes on to say "Viewing Governor Boreman as a partisan leader in 'those times that tried men's souls' even his opponents after years conceded that he possessed many high and generous qualities of both head and heart. If he struck hard blows, he did not shrink from receiving hard blows in return; and when the strife was ended he was ever ready to extend a hand, and to sink, if not forget, the past."[57]

Arthur I. Boreman, first Governor of West Virginia
Source: library.georgetown.edu

---

[57] http://www.wvculture.org/history/statehood/boremanarthur01.html

Chapter 2
John S. Carlisle – See Part I – Chapter 22

Chapter 3
Joseph Johnson -- See Part I -- Chapter 9

Chapter 4
Francis H. Pierpont, "The father of West Virginia"

Francis Pierpont was born in Morgantown in 1814. His family had deep roots in western Virginia as he was the great-great grandson of Morgan Morgan, the state's first white resident. Pierpont was the great grandson of Zackquill Morgan, founder of Morgantown.

Pierpont grew up in Fairmont and attended Allegheny College in Pennsylvania. He was a teacher and also studied law. He passed the bar exam in 1842. When the Baltimore and Ohio Railroad was seeking a right-of-way attorney in 1848, they hired Pierpont. He also was affiliated with both the Consolidated Coal Company as a partner and helped found the Fairmont Male and Female Seminary in 1856 which today is Fairmont University.

When the Commonwealth of Virginia seceded from the Union, the very pro-Union Pierpont met with others to consider action. Pierpont himself was opposed to immediate statehood which he considered unconstitutional. He became a delegate to both the First and Second Wheeling Conventions. Those conventions resulted in the formation of the Restored and Reorganized Government of Virginia and the election of Pierpont as the Governor on June 20, 1861. He was the only governor of that temporary government.

Pierpont worked tirelessly to facilitate the formation of the new state of West Virginia. Following the admission of West Virginia as a state, Pierpont's Restored and Reorganized

Government moved to Alexandria. There he governed over Virginia areas that were under Union control including parts of Northern Virginia, the Eastern shore and the Norfolk area.

Pierpont also ordered residents in Jefferson and Berkeley Counties to be allowed to vote for admission into West Virginia. With Union troops placed outside the polling places, both counties voted for inclusion into the new state of West Virginia. That vote also remains controversial even to today.

He served until after the war as provisional governor of Virginia as appointed by President Andrew Johnson and moved the state capital back to Richmond. When the President appointed a new military governor (John Schofield) for the state of Virginia, he returned to West Virginia, where he served one term in the West Virginia House of Delegates. He was also appointed collector of Internal Revenue by President James Garfield. Following his retirement from government, he became a founding member of the West Virginia Historical Society. He died March 24, 1899 and is buried in the Woodlawn Cemetery in Fairmont, West Virginia.

Francis H. Pierpont is often called "the father of West Virginia." His statue stands in Statuary Hall in the U.S. Capitol in Washington D.C. as one of only two West Virginians so honored.[58] Pierpont's statue was sculpted by Franklin Simmons in 1910. The other West Virginian so honored is John Kenna – a U.S. Senator from 1883 to 1893.

---

[58] http://www.wvhumanities.org/Statehood/pierpont.htm

Francis H. Pierpont
Source: West Virginia State Archives

Francis Harrison Pierpont statue
Statuary Hall – U.S. Capitol, Washington D.C.
http://www.aoc.gov/capitol-hill/national-statuary-hall-
collection/francis-harrison-pierpont

Chapter 5
Peter G. Van Winkle

Peter Godwin Van Winkle was born on September 7, 1808 in New York City. He studied law and became an attorney in Parkersburg, Virginia in 1835. He participated as a delegate to the 1850 constitutional convention in Virginia. He was treasurer for the Northwestern Virginia Railroad Company and later became its president.

When the secession fever was at its highest ebb, and rioters attempted to loot arms stashed in Parkersburg, Van Winkle took command of the government forces to quell the disruption. He also served as a delegate to both the First and Second Wheeling Conventions and then to the constitutional convention, supporting those who wanted to keep western Virginia in the Union.

Van Winkle became one of the first two U.S. Senators for the new state, serving from 1863-1869.

When U.S. Congress called for gradual emancipation, it didn't set well with Van Winkle. He thought that was a violation of state's rights. At the same time, he felt that he needed to put his personal agenda on hold due to the tremendous advantages that statehood had for the western Virginians. And in doing so, Van Winkle went forward in urging support of statehood.

He is most remembered after the war for breaking ranks with the Republicans in Congress when he voted to support the acquittal of President Andrew Johnson. His vote was not popular at all with either the Radical Republicans or the West Virginia legislature.

Van Winkle died in Parkersburg on April 15, 1872.

Peter J. Van Winkle
Source: <u>wvculture.org</u>

Chapter 6
Kellian Van Rensalear Whaley

Kellian Whaley was born in Utica, New York on May 6, 1821. He was a Point Pleasant, Virginia businessman specializing in lumber. When the Civil War began, Whaley became a major in the 9th West Virginia Volunteer Infantry. He was captured by the Confederate forces at Guyandotte, Virginia but escaped.

Whaley was one of the new state of West Virginia's three members of the House of Representatives serving until 1867. Congressman Whaley spoke in support of the West Virginia statehood bill in Congress on July 11, 1862.

Among his comments, Whaley said, "For eighty years have the people of West Virginia suffered from her unnatural connection with East Virginia. For nearly three generations has she petitioned and sought for the adoption of a liberal and just policy toward her. For almost a century has she borne the oppression, insult, and contumely of Eastern legislation without redress and without relief. Forty years ago, hoping for no change in policy from the Eastern aristocracy, she sought the division of the State; some contending that the Blue Ridge, and others the Alleghany mountains, should constitute the boundary. The seaboard and Piedmont districts, instead of modifying legislation and rendering it less odious to the people of West Virginia, sought to make it more permanently oppressive by detaching the valley from us, extending internal improvements of all descriptions into that section, uniting the people commercially and socially with Richmond, treating the West as her rival in commerce, her enemy, and an inferior. After the metropolitan city of Maryland had extended a branch of its road to Winchester, the Virginia Legislature denied further charters. The breeding of slaves for southern markets served also to detach the valley from the West and assimilate it to the East. Of the forty-four million dollars of State debt expended in internal improvements up to January 1,

1861, only one and a half million dollars have been expended in West Virginia. Not only has Virginia refused to permit us to improve our country, but when Baltimore proposed to build railroads through our territory at her own expense, the Legislature refused a charter."

Whaley complained that eastern Virginians had over $200,000,00 in slave property that wasn't taxable while at the same time most ever type of property in western Virginia was taxed; of constant opposition to a system of free schools and popular education; and of denial of internal improvements.

He noted that top political leaders in the state since 1776 have also been quite unfairly out of balance. He said, "Virginia has had thirty-three Governors, of whom West Virginia has had five, and twenty-four United States Senators, of which West Virginia has had but three."

But Whaley said the greatest disparity was "called the 'mixed basis of representation.' In the west portion of the State there exists a large majority of white population, and in the other portion the slave property interest, and giving rise to diversity of sentiment. The East insists upon protection of property by apportionment of representation; that the majority of the people should not rule, but the majority of interests; that the great wealth of the State is in slaves, and that the forty thousand slaveholders of the East should rule; that while eight hundred and ninety-eight thousand people have, say fifty representatives, $495,000 of taxes must also have fifty representatives; that slavery, and not free white men, is the element of political power; that more than one hundred and twenty-five thousand citizens of the West are properly denied representation in the councils of the State; that, with an immense majority of free white men in the West, the legislative power is rightly placed in the hands of the minority, giving them thirty majority on joint ballot in General Assembly, as Mr. Scott said in the Virginia convention, 'to secure property [slaves] by not surrendering the legislative control to a majority of mere numbers.'"

After President Lincoln's assassination, Whaley had the honor of serving on the Congressional committee that accompanied the body of President Lincoln on the funeral train back to Springfield, Illinois. Whaley also served on the Committee on Invalid Pensions, the Committee on Revolutionary Claims, and as a customs collector in Texas. Whaley died in Point Pleasant, West Virginia on May 20, 1876 and is buried in Lone Oak Cemetery in Point Pleasant.

Kellian Van Rensalear Whaley
Source: wvculture.org

Chapter 7
Waitman T. Willey

Waitman T. Willey was born in a log cabin in Mason County near Farmington, Virginia (today West Virginia) in 1811. He settled in Morgantown following his graduation from Madison College in Uniontown, Pennsylvania.

Following his service as Clerk of the Court of Monongalia County (1841-1852) Willey ran unsuccessfully for Congress. His early political service included being a delegate to the Virginia Constitutional Convention in 1850-51. At those long heated discussions, Willey argued that the elite land owners in the eastern section of the state had dominated the state's politics for way too long. And that it was time to revert to a fairer system of representation.

He was also a delegate to the Virginia Secession Convention in April, 1861 when the Commonwealth of Virginia voted to secede from the Union. Being a loyal Unionist, Willey warned his fellow delegates that a vote for secession would "dissolve the state." Whereas Willey and most of his colleagues from western Virginia voted against secession, the majority voted for secession. On April 17, 1861, Virginia seceded from the Union. Willey and the other western Virginia delegates left disappointedly following the secession vote.

It didn't take long for Willey and the others to organize meetings on their own. Willey proposed that the western Virginia counties declare the Richmond government illegitimate. They favored reorganizing the state.

He was very active in the First Wheeling Convention for statehood.

A Morgantown attorney, Willey became one of the first two West Virginia U.S. Senators. Peter G. Van Winkle was the other U.S. Senator. Willey served in the U.S. Senate representing both Virginia (July 9, 1861 – March 4, 1863) and West Virginia (August 4, 1863 – March 4, 1871). When he represented the Restored and Reorganized Government of Virginia, he had replaced Virginia Senator James M. Mason, who had resigned when the state seceded from the Union.

While in the U.S. Senate, Willey proposed the amendment (the Willey Amendment) that called for all slaves younger than twenty-one years old on July 4, 1863 to become free when they reached their 21st birthday. It was interesting that it was Willey, a former slave owner, who offered the compromise on the question of freedom for the new state's Negroes that assured West Virginia's approval for statehood. And it was Willey's petition to Congress, presented on May 29, 1862, that eventually led to West Virginia's statehood.

Willey lived in the Waitman T. Willey House in Morgantown. That house is on the National Register of Historic Places. Mr. Willey died on May 2, 1900 in Morgantown.

The Philadelphia Inquirer once called Willey a "tall, fine, spectacled specimen of the old Virginia gentleman."

Waitman T. Willey
Source: gathkinsons.net

Acknowledgements

I am grateful to the West Virginia newspapers who agreed to publish my 27 part series on West Virginia statehood that led to the publishing of this book.

A special thanks to the West Virginia Division of Culture and History (www.wvculture.org) that has always maintained a huge amount of historical information, documents, and photographs concerning West Virginia statehood. They are an incredibly valuable resource for any studies on this subject. Without their resources, no book of this type could have ever been attempted.

Thanks, as always, to my family, friends, and supporters all over the country. Your encouragement has been totally awesome.

I am eternally grateful to my teachers in my early years who continually told me that my writing was good and that someday I might be a writer.

I could not be who I am today on any level without the love from my parents, both now overseeing my life from front row seats in heaven.

And finally thanks to Rebecca S. Boreczky, the teacher who nudge me into publishing. I am continually grateful that you helped start me on this amazing journey.